IN A ZEN GARDEN

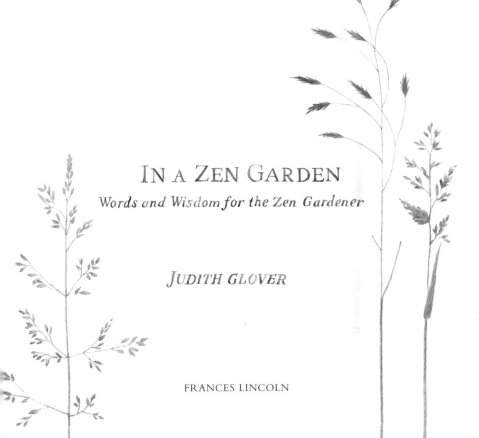

In a Zen Garden

Words and Wisdom for the Zen Gardener

Judith Glover

FRANCES LINCOLN

For my Mother and Father

CONTENTS

GO beyond this way
or that way,
to the farther shore
where the world dissolves
and everything
becomes clear.
Beyond this shore
and the farther shore,
beyond the beyond,
where there is
no beginning,
no end,
without fear
go.

The Buddha

Part 1.
THE SPIRIT OF ZEN

Zen Buddhism originated in Korea and first came to Japan from China in the 6th century. Zen holds that meditation is a vital tool in the search for self-knowledge and the early Zen gardens were created to provide a harmonious environment for this silent contemplation. In order to achieve the state of 'no mind' that Zen aspires to, riddles known as 'koans' were devised. Through contemplating their meanings it becomes possible to free one's mind from limiting and preconditioned thought patterns.

Shinto, the indigenous faith of the Japanese, also lays great emphasis on meditation and over the centuries the two faiths came to co-exist peacefully together within Japanese culture and everyday life. In essence, Shinto is the celebration of nature. Unusually shaped rocks or trees are accorded special respect and are endowed with holy qualities. Shinto gods, known as 'kami', take the form of wind, rain, mountains, trees or rivers. The spirits of animals and all living things are revered.

During the Heian period (794–1185) the Chinese science of Feng Shui was introduced into Japan. Feng Shui literally means 'wind and water' and its exponents believe that unseen natural forces run like magnetic currents throughout the world. The forces are Yin and Yang, negative and positive, male and female, darkness and light. It is through the precise balancing of these energies within the surroundings that perfect harmony can be achieved.

Over decades of dedicated thought Zen gardens have evolved to incorporate elements from these overlapping, complementary beliefs. The complexity of these abstract ideas can be hard to grasp. Our hearts must be open and our minds clear of all prejudice to fully benefit from the tranquillity and peace a Zen garden will provide.

Surrender yourself to stillness,
the truth you seek is already there...

Not the stillness is stillness,
but the stillness in movement
is the real stillness.

Give complete attention to
the detail of every action
you perform.
This process is meditation.
Self and thoughts are forgotten,
your mind is clear of all limitation.

Realise the moment

focus on the task at hand

'Mindfulness' is to pay equal attention to all things, whether significant or insignificant. Apply this principle to every detail of your garden.

Become one with nature, then follow its requests...

Celebrate the beauty
of natural chance and the
perfection of man~made
things, the rational and the
random, the fusion of
opposites.

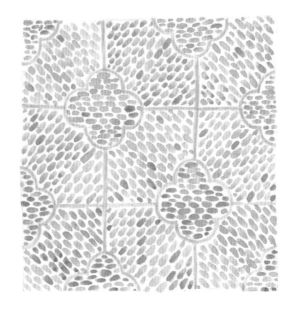

Let your mind become like
a polished mirror, reflecting
every detail of your passing
life, yet remaining unchanged.

Gradually you will achieve tranquillity.

The flux of life will seem
as ripples
on the surface
of changelessness.

THINK of the beauty of living nature the mountains and waters of the natural landscape.

From the Sakuteiki – 'The Way of Gardening'

Part 2.

THE ZEN GARDEN

Towards the end of the Heian period the principles of Zen gardening were formally compiled in a manual called the *Sakuteiki* (*The Way of Gardening*). This is the earliest known garden manual in existence. It taught the Zen gardener to study the natural landscape at its most beautiful and similarly to create a garden in harmony with its surroundings, composed with plants, trees and shrubs suited to the given climate and conditions. Unlike Western gardens, with their colourful, changing displays of annual and perennial flowers, a Zen garden strives to be true to the essence of Nature.

Therefore, if your garden is shady and wet, rather than attempting to create a lawn, allow moss to clothe the ground. Instead of struggling with plants that require sunshine to prosper, introduce shade-loving plants, such as ferns and hostas, that will thrive in dappled light.

In sterile, dry conditions, where many plants will fail, a 'karesansui' garden of raked sand, symbolizing flowing water, will give a refreshing atmosphere of energy and movement. Rocks are an essential component of all dry gardens, often positioned in groups of three, five or seven, designed to represent mountains, lakes and islands. Water is always present in some form even if, as in a gravel garden, it is there only metaphorically. In the tiniest gardens, where there is room for nothing more than a lantern and a few rocks and plants, a stone 'chozubachi' (hand basin) will introduce the presence of water.

A Zen garden has a static, unchanging quality that is achieved through a predominance of evergreen plants, carefully maintained through constant pruning. Within this framework of muted colours and solid structure the impact of seasonal changes becomes acutely defined, and flowering shrubs, spring blossom or autumn leaves all become symbolic of their season.

Whilst it is not vital to 'understand', it is essential to 'feel' these principles so that the spirit of Zen will flourish in your garden.

SHOTOKU NO SANSUI
'mountain water of living nature'

Seek inspiration in the natural landscape
at its most beautiful and create
your garden in its likeness.

KOHAN NI SHITAGAU
'follow the request'

Be guided by the
natural spirit of the
site and strive for an inner
stillness within which
to 'hear' the request.

SHAKKEI
'borrowed landscape'

Study the surroundings
and take advantage
of all favourable aspects.

SUCHIGAETE
'off balance, asymmetry'

Position rocks, ponds and features
asymmetrically within the symmetry
of man-made boundaries.

This will create a sense of balance and harmony.

FUZEI
'a breeze of feeling'

Be sensitive to the atmosphere of the garden

but, equally, listen to your own aesthetic tastes

so that your spirit too will be reflected.

Lilium 'Brushmarks'

Lilium 'Corsage'

Lilium 'Harmony'

Do what you are doing while you are doing it.
When the work is done, put away the tools.
Leave no trace.

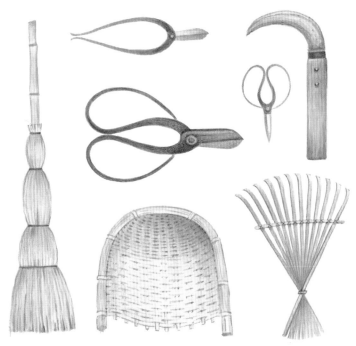

The action and the goal exist as one.

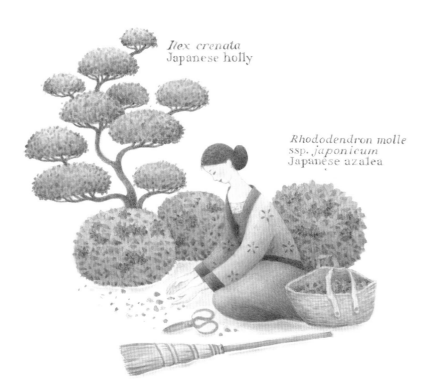

Ilex crenata
Japanese holly

Rhododendron molle
ssp. *japonicum*
Japanese azalea

Water is the source of life
and symbol of purity.

In a Zen garden it is
always present in some form.

KARESANSUI
'dry-landscape garden'

KARE~NEGARE
'dry stream'

GINSHANADA
'silver sand, open sea'

Zen is a reverence for the
beauty of natural materials.

YOTSUME GATI
Lattice fences made from
bamboo and wooden boards
arranged to create subtle
geometric patterns.

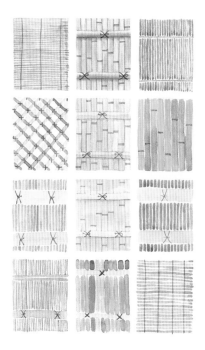

Rocks, stone, gravel and
sand are all essential
components.

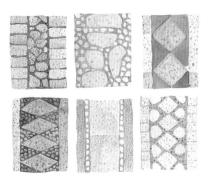

Natural objects aquire an
individual significance and
a symbolic dimension when
given a name.

Rock of
Spirit
Kings

Garden by the
Winding Stream

Rock of Ten
Thousand
Eons

Seat of Restfulness

Trees and evergreen shrubs give colour, form and texture,

Prunus × subhirtella 'Autumnalis'

Pinus parviflora

Acer palmatum 'Osakazuki'

flower~beds would detract from the quiet beauty they provide.

Prunus × subhirtella 'Pendula',

Fargesia nitida

Ilex crenata 'Golden Tip',

The timeless, unchanging character of the Zen garden is preserved through careful pruning.

'COMPACT' PRUNING

Small-leaved evergreen shrubs, clipped into regular spheres.

Buxus sempervirens

'MASS' PRUNING

Several shrubs planted together and shaped to suggest rolling hills, stormy seas or islands in the ocean.

Lonicera nitida

'CLOUD' PRUNING

Trees or large shrubs trained to suggest billowing clouds.

Cupressus arizonica

'LINEAR' PRUNING

Trees or large shrubs pruned to reveal the structure of their trunks and branches.

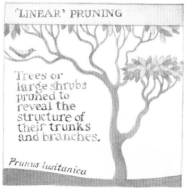

Prunus lusitanica

Mono no aware
'sensitivity towards beings'

Become attuned to the needs of
your garden and the plants and
creatures within it.

Then you will be at one with QUI,
the vital breath of the universe.

WHEN you hear
the splash of the
water drops
that fall into
the stone bowl,
you will feel that
all the dust
of your mind
is washed
away.

Sen-No-Rikyu. Zen Tea Master

Part 3.

OUTSIDE ~ INSIDE

Ikebana and Bonsai

Early Japanese palace temples were designed so that the outside linked seamlessly with the inside. Sliding screens opened to reveal the landscape and wooden floors extended outwards from the internal rooms on to verandas from which to view and reach the garden.

Ikebana – the art of flower composition – was practised to further accentuate the close connection between Man and Nature and to draw attention to the changing seasons. Each arrangement would be placed on a 'tokonoma', a niche used for the display of cherished possessions. Here, for its short lifetime, it would become the treasured focal point of the room. A single brilliantly coloured autumn bough would be looked upon with as much reverence as the most precious object.

The earliest form of ikebana was based on harmonious groupings of three, symbolizing the trinity of forces – horizontal, diagaonal and vertical – representing Heaven, Earth and Man.

Through the centuries, though many styles of ikebana have evolved, the guiding principles remain the same. Arrangements must be simple, understated and restrained, and there must be a harmonious relationship between the materials, the container and the setting.

Bonsai – the art of miniaturizing trees, shrubs or vines through careful training – was introduced from China to Japan during the Kamakura period (1185–1333). Given proper care bonsai can live for hundreds of years, their evolving beauty representing an unbroken link with the past. Bonsai are kept outside and are brought inside for display only at special times of the year, either to draw attention to the season or to mark the flower festival that they have come to symbolize.

Bonsai should always appear natural, like miniature trees, displaying the effects of time and weather, admired for their age and revered as reminders of those who have nurtured them before us.

KADO
'the way of the flower'

Ikebana seeks to express
the essence of the material
and to reflect

the rhythms

and order

of

nature.

FLOWERS ARE AN EXPRESSION OF JOY ~ LOOK ON THEM WITH LOVE

Japanese
flowering
quince

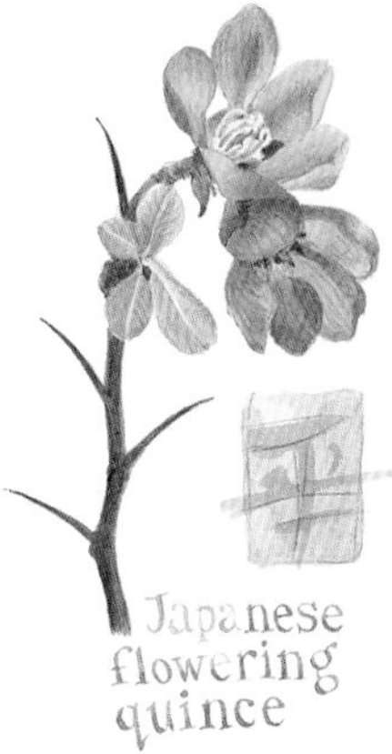

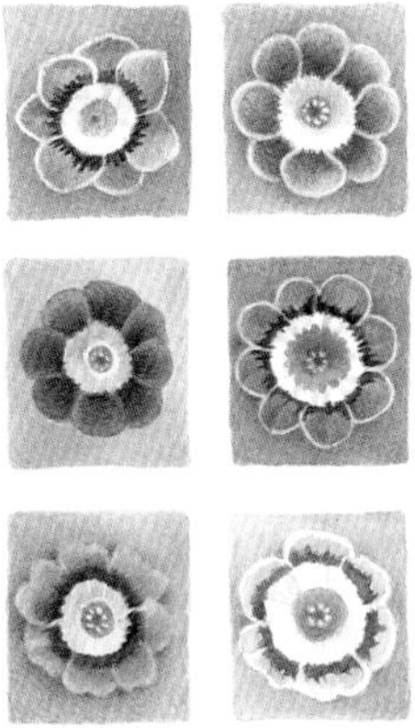

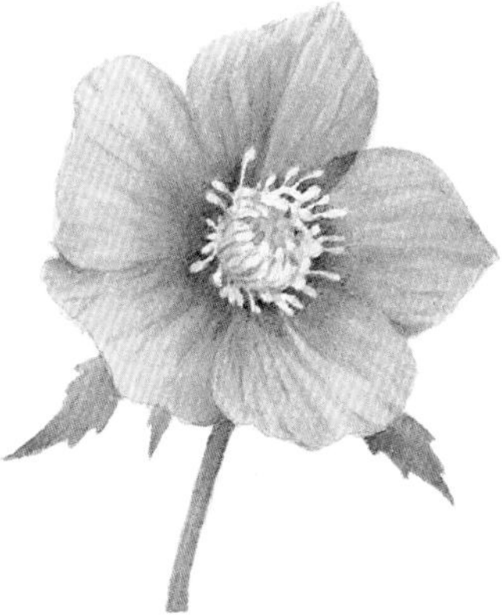

HANA~NO~KOKORO
'flower heart'

There is unspoken communication
between the artist and the
material.

Anemone hupehensis var. *japonica*

Ikebana and meditation become the same.

Equal importance is given
to flowerless branches
as to prized blooms.

Withered leaves, grasses,
berries, seed heads and buds
are valued as highly as
flowers.

HEIKA

Arrangements
in tall vases
with narrow
openings.

MORIBANA

Arrangements
in low, shallow
containers with
wide openings.

TEN
HEAVEN

JIN
MAN

EARTH CHI

TEN ~ CHI ~ JIN
'Heaven ~ earth ~ man'

A tall, upright
central stem
accompanied by
two shorter stems
symbolizes the
relationship
between heaven,
earth and man.

IKEBANA
CELEBRATES
THE
BEAUTY
OF
OMISSION

Empty space is an essential element of the composition.

Bonsai are created with skill,
patience and care, yet
show no trace of human
intervention.

Malus halliana
Flowering crabapple

Man and nature in harmony.

MAN
AND
NATURE
AS
ONE

Salix babylonica
Weeping willow

SPRING has its hundred flowers,
Autumn has its many moons.
Summer has cool winds, Winter has snow.
If useless thoughts do not cloud your mind,
Each day is the best of your life.

Wu Men Hui Kai (1183-1260)

Part 4.

MUJOKAN

Night of Endless Dreams

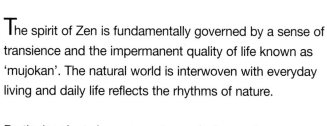

The spirit of Zen is fundamentally governed by a sense of transience and the impermanent quality of life known as 'mujokan'. The natural world is interwoven with everyday living and daily life reflects the rhythms of nature.

Particular plants have come to symbolize each season. *Prunus mume* (Japanese apricot) and *Adonis amurensis* both bloom before the last snows have melted and herald the end of winter. *Sakura*, the flowering cherry and national flower of Japan, follows in profusion – its brief flowering time so glorious that it is taken to symbolize a glimpse of Heaven or the perfection of youth. In the month of April on Mount Yoshino in Nara, 100,000 cherry trees blossom and 'hanami' (flower viewing parties) take place in celebration. In a Zen garden, however, a single flowering tree signifies not only the arrival of spring, but new life, renewal and the fleeting nature of time.

Japanese summers are long and hot so the predominantly green Zen garden is a calm refuge from the city streets and busy lives.

Ponds and lakes are edged with *Iris ensata* (Japanese water iris), and humming insects, dragonflies and butterflies fill the air. Cooling winds blow through thickets of bamboo and the sound of rustling grasses soothes the senses. Blue and mauve flowers of *Ipomea*, the twining morning glory vine, add short-lived splashes of vivid colour.

Autumn is a season very close to the Japanese heart. Chrysanthemums and the flowering grass *Miscanthus sinensis* are among its symbolic plants. These, and brilliantly coloured maple leaves, mark the onset of winter and bring a wistful note of sadness – Man at one with Nature, Man the same as Nature.

In winter, evergreen trees and shrubs provide form and structure. 'Hatsuhana' – the blobs of snow on the bare tree branches – are known as 'the first flowers', until the early blooms of *Camellia sasanqua* appear and the annual cycle begins once again.

To the Zen gardener, the natural world
is inseparably interwoven with
everyday living.

SAKURA
'cherry blossom'

Flower of spring. Symbol of
new life and renewal.

There is a connection
between the passing
of the seasons and
the unfolding of
human life.

Cherry

SUMMER

Morning Glory

AUTUMN

Chrysanthemum

WINTER

Camellia

The changing seasons
reflect the dream-like
quality of our own
existence.

Iris ensata
Japanese water iris

Beauty is found in the transience
of all things.

Cercidiphyllum japonicum
Katsura tree

Graceful deciduous tree
with rounded heart-shaped
leaves that turn brilliant
shades of yellow, orange
and red in autumn and
smell of burnt sugar when
touched by the first frosts.

Liriodendron chinensis
Chinese tulip tree

Large, deciduous tree with curiously shaped leaves and brilliant golden foliage in the autumn.

Ginkgo biloba
Maidenhair tree

Distinctive, fan~shaped leaves and brilliant golden foliage in the autumn.

Nandina domestica
Heavenly bamboo

Elegant foliage and jewel~like scarlet berries that ripen in the depth of winter.

Everything will change
of its own accord
Nothing is constant,
everything is in a
state of flux.

SHO~CHIKU~BAI
'The three friends of winter'

Pine, bamboo, plum.

P
i
N
E

B
A
M
B
O
O

P
L
U
M

Revered
for its
unchanging
appearance.
Symbol of
longevity
and
happiness.

Retains its
leaves in
winter~
symbol
of strength
and
honesty.

Blooms before
the last snows
have left the
ground~
symbol of
new hope.

TSURU SHIMA
'Crane island'

Mythical island of immortality~

Metaphor for the migration of the soul to Heaven

What is it that remains
when there is no longer
the self?

Everything, and you are part of everything.

Frances Lincoln Ltd
4 Torriano Mews
Torriano Avenue
London NW5 2RZ
www.franceslincoln.com

A catalogue record for this book is available from
the British Library.

ISBN 0 7112 2438 2

Printed and bound in Singapore
by Star Standard.

First Frances Lincoln edition 2005

2 4 6 8 9 7 5 3 1